VIOLENCE AS ENTERTAINMENT

WHY AGGRESSION SELLS

by Erika Wittekind

Content Consultant: John V. Pavlik,
Professor and Chair, Department of Journalism and Media Studies,
School of Communication and Information, Rutgers University

COMPASS POINT BOOKS
a capstone imprint

EXPLORING
MEDIA LITERACY

Compass Point Books
1710 Roe Crest Drive
North Mankato, MN 56003

Editors: Mari Kesselring and Lauren Coss
Designers: Becky Daum and Kazuko Collins

Image Credits
Eric Jamison/AP Images, cover, 46; George Cairns/iStockphoto, back cover (left);
Anatoliy Babiy/iStockphoto, back cover (center); Marcello Farina/Shutterstock
Images, back cover (right); Nicholas Piccillo/Shutterstock Images, 5; Sony Pictures/
Photofest, 6; Kevin Higley/AP Images, 8; Paul Sakuma/AP Images, 11, 73; Red Line
Editorial, 12, 39, 48, 64; Paul Drinkwater/NBCU Photo Bank/AP Images, 13; William
Casey/Shutterstock Images, 14; Monkey Business Images/Shutterstock Images, 16;
Shutterstock Images, 18; Wellphoto/Shutterstock Images, 21; iStockphoto, 23, 40,
75; M&N/Alamy, 25; Everett Collection Inc/Alamy, 28; Camerique/Getty Images, 29;
Andrew Cooper/Miramax Films/Photofest, 31; Thomas Pajot/Bigstock, 32; Patricia
Marroquin/Bigstock, 35 (top); Andrew Rich/iStockphoto, 35 (bottom); Walt Disney
Pictures/Photofest, 37; Photofest, 38; Warner Bros. Pictures/Photofest, 41; Tom Young/
iStockphoto, 42; Supri Suharjoto/Shutterstock Images, 43; Carl Ballou/Shutterstock
Images, 45; Jason DeCrow/AP Images, 49; Karen Struthers/Shutterstock Images, 51;
Jamie Cross/Bigstock, 52; Warner Bros./Photofest, 55; Tim Newman/iStockphoto, 56;
Anton Albert/Shutterstock Images, 59 (top); Brandon Alms/iStockphoto, 59 (bottom),
62, 71; Paolo Scarlata/iStockphoto, 60; Barone Firenze/Shutterstock Images, 65; Ric
Francis/AP Images, 67; Blend Images/Shutterstock Images, 68; Rich Pedroncelli/AP
Images, 69; WaveBreak Media Ltd/Shutterstock Images, 70

Design Elements: Becky Daum/Red Line Editorial

Library of Congress Cataloging-in-Publication Data
Wittekind, Erika, 1980–
  Violence as entertainment : why aggression sells / by Erika Wittekind.
    p. cm.—(Exploring media literacy)
  Includes bibliographical references and index.
  ISBN 978-0-7565-4520-8 (library binding)
  ISBN 978-0-7565-4536-9 (paperback)
  1. Violence in mass media—Juvenile literature. 2. Mass media—Social aspects—
Juvenile literature. 3. Mass media—Influence—Juvenile literature. I. Title.
  P96.V5W58 2012
  303.6—dc23   2011038006

Visit Compass Point Books on the Internet at *www.capstonepub.com*

Printed in the United States of America in Stevens Point, Wisconsin.
012013   007118R

CONTENTS

CHAPTER 1

ENTERTAINMENT MEETS REAL LIFE

> "We live in a violent society. Art imitates the modes of life, not the other way around. It would be better ... to clean up society than to clean up the reflection of that society."
>
> —Zev Braun, CBS TV executive

Do you enjoy horror movies or superhero comics? Do you listen to music with lyrics about violence? Do you like to watch crime shows on TV? Join the crowd. Many people enjoy such forms of entertainment. They might awe over the special effects or experience a thrill at seeing a car chase or shoot-out. They might seek out music with violent themes as a way of expressing their own anger or sadness. Video games involving shooting or killing can seem exciting or fun, even if real-life acts of violence seem frightening or immoral.

Depictions of violence have become increasingly common in today's world.

While conflict has been a part of popular culture since the invention of storytelling, modern technology has made that content more accessible than ever. Not only is violent content seen on TV and on movie screens, but it can be downloaded as videos and heard in MP3s. Video games featuring violence provide hours of entertainment. What's more, modern programming techniques and special effects have made the blood and gore more realistic than ever before.

Research in the 1970s showed that children saw more than 11,000 homicides on TV by age 14. If that number sounds high, consider this: More recent studies have found that children see approximately 10,000 acts of violence depicted on TV each *year*.

Is viewing violent entertainment harmless? Or does it affect people in ways they don't even realize? This question has concerned parents, experts, politicians, and the media for years. As such a critical

Children are often excited to see the latest superhero films, but movies such as *Spider-Man 2* contain a lot of violence as well as heroism. ·····················

social question, it makes sense to examine issues that surround violence as entertainment. Why do audiences enjoy violence so much? Does exposure to so much fake violence have any relation to real acts of aggression? How does the violent nature of so much entertainment affect people? And if it is harmful, what should be done about it?

A Violent Tragedy

In 1999 two teenagers in Littleton, Colorado, shocked the world when they walked into their high school and opened fire. They killed 12 students and one teacher at Columbine High School, then took their own lives. Twenty-four people were injured.

In 1999 two teenagers in Littleton, Colorado, shocked the world when they walked into their high school and opened fire.

As they were trying to make sense of the tragedy, the media quickly zeroed in on the fact that the killers had enjoyed playing a violent video game—*Doom*. One journalist, John Leo of *U.S. News and World Report*, described the crime scene as resembling a video game. He wrote: "Note the cool and casual cruelty, the outlandish arsenal of weapons, the cheering and laughing while hunting down victims one by one. All of this seems to reflect the style and feel of the video killing games they played so often."

Like many others Leo found disturbing the number of children who spend their time playing violent video games. While most understand the difference between fantasy and reality, some children are emotionally vulnerable. They may have been mistreated. They may be working out their

The fact that the shooters at Columbine High School were known to play violent video games brought national attention to the issue of violence in the media.

feelings of anger and rejection on an Xbox, a Wii, or a Playstation. A few of them might even end up carrying out violent acts in real life.

PROFILE OF A KILLER

People who commit violent acts aren't always people who are already interested in violence. The U.S. Secret Service conducted a study of non-gang-related school shootings that occurred between 1974 and 2000. The purpose of the study was to determine if any particular profile for the students involved could be developed to aid in the identification of warning signs. The study found that more than half of the attackers had an interest in violent movies, video games, music, or books. However, no one particular interest was found to be common among all the various incidents. The largest number of offenders—more than one-third—had expressed an interest in violence through their own writings or artwork, as opposed to movies or games.

Considering Violence and Aggression

Events such as school shootings bring violence in the media into the forefront of our minds. However, this has been an issue of much debate for decades. New technologies have made all forms of media, including those that feature acts of violence, more prominent in our lives. Media violence is frequently defined as any depiction of a threat of

Media violence is frequently defined as any depiction of a threat of force or actual use of force to harm someone.

force or actual use of force to harm someone. Experts disagree whether to include verbal acts of aggression in this definition. Many studies have shown a link between media violence and real aggression. The aggression can show itself in attitudes, words, or actions. It can appear soon after exposure to media violence. Or it can contribute to aggression displayed later in life. One long-term study showed that young people who watch more than seven hours of TV a week were more likely to commit an aggressive act later in life than their peers who spent less time watching TV.

In the past few decades movies have become more graphic. Video games have become more realistic. Aggression also appears in music lyrics, comic books, and other forms of entertainment. This makes some worry about the exposure people have to so much violence and the potential consequences of it. Is there anything wrong with enjoying a movie featuring a bloody shoot-out or playing a game that rewards players for killing? Does repeated exposure to this kind of entertainment

More than 6 million copies of *Grand Theft Auto IV*,
a video game with violent themes, were sold in
the first week of sales alone. ⋯⋯⋯⋯⋯⋯⋯⋯⋯⋯⋯⋯⋯⋯⋯⋯

desensitize people, making them care less about
real violence? What other effects can media have
on feelings and behavior?

Not all popular video games are violent. However, violent video games do sell well. A 2008 survey found *Grand Theft Auto* to be one of the most popular games. But *Guitar Hero*, which is nonviolent, was the most popular game.

10 Most Frequently Played Games

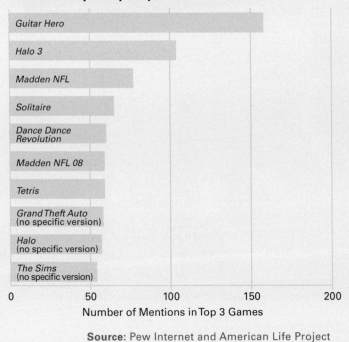

Number of Mentions in Top 3 Games

Source: Pew Internet and American Life Project

Placing Blame

In the wake of the Columbine shootings, some blame was directed at controversial singer Marilyn

Marilyn Manson is known for being a controversial performer. He performs what is known as shock rock and implements violent elements into his shows.

Manson. This was despite the fact that the shooters were not fans of his music. Manson has been criticized for exposing young people to dark themes

Some people worry that teens who listen to music with violent themes might be more likely to be involved in violence at school. ·

such as suicide or violence. Following the negative attention he received after the Columbine tragedy, Manson wrote an opinion piece in *Rolling Stone* magazine. In it Manson criticized the media for making entertainment providers a scapegoat instead of delving into more complicated problems such as the access children have to guns. He also spoke out against people who dislike something merely because it is different. He pointed out that some of his music has been misunderstood. For example, one song that some interpreted as promoting gun violence, "Lunchbox," was actually about his experience being picked on at recess. While his music is controversial, Manson said he does not support violence as a solution. "Sometimes music, movies and books are the only things that let us feel like someone else feels like we do," he wrote for *Rolling Stone*. "I've always tried to let people know it's OK, or better, if you don't fit into the program."

Other artists have also come under fire for tackling the subject of violence in their music. The song "Jeremy" by Pearl Jam is about a social outcast who commits suicide at school. The music video, produced in 1995, doesn't show the gun. Instead it focuses on the faces of the blood-spattered classmates who witness the suicide. The year after the "Jeremy" video was made, a 14-year-old boy who had seen it killed his teacher and two classmates in Moses Lake, Washington. The boy's defense attorneys said he was influenced by the Pearl Jam video. The boy was

The year after the "Jeremy" video was made, a 14-year-old boy who had seen it killed his teacher and two classmates in Moses Lake, Washington.

Bullying can happen at school, at the playground, and even on the Internet. Some people think musicians who write violent lyrics draw attention to the dangers of bullying. ·

mentally ill, had been bullied, and came from a troubled family. These factors made him particularly vulnerable to the music video's violent content, they claimed. However, the jury found the boy guilty and sentenced him to life in prison.

Some people worry about the impact videos such as "Jeremy" have on vulnerable children who may end up acting out what they've seen. Others think bands perform a service by drawing attention to the dangers of bullying. And many people think that regardless of the impact, music and music videos are forms of expression that should not be limited.

Sociologist Karen Sternheimer argued that just because violence is the subject of music does not mean the music promotes violence. She wrote: "Instead of trying to understand why some people find solace in Marilyn Manson's music or consider the very real problem of bullying and alienation, we often choose to blame the music and to fear acts like Manson and their fans."

Sternheimer points out that the negative reactions to such artists and their fans can even increase those feelings of rejection and lead those fans to feel more like outcasts.

Is There a Link?

More than 1,000 studies have supported the link between exposure to violence in the media and aggressive feelings and behavior in children. These studies have found that such content can desensitize people to real violence. This makes them less likely to help people who have been hurt. Exposure to violent content can increase the likelihood that children see physical or verbal aggression as an acceptable solution to a conflict. Seeing so much fake violence also can create feelings of mistrust or paranoia. Based on what children see on TV or in a movie theater, they might develop the impression that the world is a very dangerous place. In some cases viewing violence may even contribute to actual violence.

Some studies have found that young children who see violent movies or TV shows or play violent video games are more likely to show physical or verbal aggression later in life. This is especially true when the media violence is realistic or goes unpunished. These effects are most pronounced from playing violent video games because of their interactive nature.

Of course, what children watch or what games they play are not the only factors that determine how they will act. While violent video games may be one factor in youth violence, real-life experiences and emotions

Media violence is not only found in adult crime shows or R-rated movies. While some children do see such content, many children are also exposed to violence in children's shows or movies. Research has found that more than half of TV shows feature violence, and 70 percent of prime-time shows do. Shows intended for children actually show more violence, although the actions are characterized differently from adult shows. A prime-time show has an average of five violent acts per hour, compared to 20 violent acts per hour of children's programming.

In shows such as *Power Rangers*, heroes are shown using violence to achieve a goal. Often violence is depicted as funny and is less likely to involve weapons than on prime-time shows. Among children's shows, slapstick and superhero cartoons feature the most violence. Shows that focus on relationships and public television programming contain the least amount of violence.

also play a role. Children who have been bullied, abused, mistreated, or feel depressed or alienated may be more likely to act violently. They also may be more interested in violent entertainment. Some have concluded that while violence in the media is not the only factor, it does contribute to violent behavior and can even act as a trigger that sets off a violent act.

Some have concluded that while violence in the media is not the only factor, it does contribute to violent behavior and can even act as a trigger that sets off a violent act.

Other experts see interest in violent entertainment as an expression of an aggressive tendency rather than its direct cause. Some believe that focusing too much on the issue of media violence may actually be harmful. They say it lessens the focus on more significant but complicated problems such as bullying in schools, child abuse, gun control, or gang violence.

An Ongoing Debate

The effects of violence in entertainment are frequently debated following school shootings or other incidents of violence involving children. Do you think the media focus too much or too little on this aspect? What other factors might be at play in such a tragedy?

Do you think songs about problems such as bullying, alienation, and suicide are harmful or helpful? Do you ever listen to music that contains sad or angry lyrics? Why do you listen to it? Does listening to the music affect your emotions or behavior? How do you think such music might affect other people?

Experts disagree on the actual effects of media violence, such as playing games with realistic video game controllers. Some think it can lead to more aggressive behavior or a greater tolerance for violent acts. Others think there are other, more significant factors that contribute to school violence. ·

CHAPTER 2

FROM GLADIATORS TO COWBOYS

> "Violence in entertainment is as old as entertainment itself. The Romans delighted in watching Christians do battle with hungry lions. Dramatic theater—from the ancient Greeks to Shakespeare to Andrew Lloyd Webber—has always been thick with jealousy, retribution, and violence."
>
> —Douglas A. Gentile, editor of Media Violence and Children: A Complete Guide for Parents and Professionals

People have been using violence as entertainment for centuries, even millennia. Concerns about how representations of violence affect people, especially children, have existed for just as long. Duels and murders were common to the plots of the Greek tragedies in the 400s BC. Plato, a Greek philosopher of the time, worried about the effects of this violence on the children who viewed the plays. In the centuries following

the invention of the printing press in the 1400s, newspapers and books could be made and acquired more cheaply and rapidly. This gave the working class more options and the upper class less control over information. The more popular novels became, the more fear grew over regulating their content. Violent themes were also a concern in England. During the 1800s young men had more free time to enjoy the theater and literature. Some critics blamed this youth culture for increased crime.

From the late 1800s to approximately 1915, dime novels were a very popular form of American entertainment. These inexpensive books often featured Western themes and depicted gunfights or battles between cowboys and American Indians. By the 1930s comic books were becoming increasingly popular in the United States. Comic books were colorful, cheap, and easy to acquire. They told

GLADIATORS

Most violence in entertainment today is simulated, but ancient Romans found entertainment in real violence. Gladiatorial games were popular from approximately the 300s BC to the 200s BC. Gladiators were trained fighters, most of whom were slaves, prisoners of war, or criminals who had no choice but to participate. Romans gathered at arenas to watch the gladiators duel each other, often to the death. When a gladiator was wounded, the crowd had the option of ending the game or letting the game continue until his death. As Christianity became more widespread, criticism of the games mounted. Emperor Constantine I outlawed the games in AD 325.

While spectators no longer flock to arenas to see someone killed, some people have drawn parallels to modern-day sports, such as boxing. Matches are won either by knocking out an opponent or by earning points for landing punches. The violent sport was outlawed in some countries in the 1800s. But its popularity has led to its acceptance today. Still, even with stricter rules, boxers have died from injuries sustained in matches.

exciting adventure, superhero, or crime stories. The popularity of comic books continued at the same time as McCarthyism in the 1950s. This was a

During the 1950s comic books geared toward children and young adults often depicted scenes of gunfights and battles between cowboys and American Indians.

time in U.S. history when officials were focused on suppressing communism and other ideas that were viewed as contrary to U.S. interests. This created an atmosphere of fear about preserving the national culture. While comic books had nothing to do with communism, some people viewed their sometimes-violent stories as a threat.

Crime comics, which told stories of murder, theft, and other criminal activity, were particularly troublesome to some psychiatrists. They reported that such depictions of violence could lead to violent behavior in children. Approximately 50 cities attempted to ban the sale of crime comics. Critics unsuccessfully tried to get Congress to pass a law limiting these comics' production. A Senate subcommittee conducted hearings on the matter in 1954. This led to the development of the Comics Code Authority. Through this organization, members of the comic book industry set their own rules and rating system. The Comics Code Authority disbanded in 2011 when the last of its members dropped out.

The Rise of Motion Pictures

Movies started to gain prominence in the 1900s. Early motion pictures were viewed at small theaters called nickelodeons, because admission cost a nickel. Approximately 10,000 nickelodeons were spread across the United States by 1910. As they gained popularity, newspapers denounced

COMICS CODE AUTHORITY

The Comics Code Authority was created in 1954 in response to hearings of the Senate Subcommittee on Juvenile Delinquency. Under scrutiny, the comic book publishers decided to establish their own rules governing content. These rules were self-enforced. At first words such as "horror" or "terror" could not be used in titles. Crime could not be portrayed in a positive light. Depictions of vampires, ghouls, cannibals, and werewolves were discouraged, although later the rules allowed for stories based on classic literature, such as *Dracula* or *Frankenstein*. In 2001 Marvel Comics decided to use its own rating system. Other comic book companies followed suit until 2011 when the Comics Code Authority disbanded.

them as hazardous to American children. They reported that children who saw movies were likely to run away from home, steal, or become burglars. But these stories were based on a few cases rather than on extensive data. Such concerns led to the creation of the National Board of Censorship of Motion Pictures, a self-regulating body within the industry. The board was an early version of modern ratings organizations.

Nickelodeon theaters were criticized in the early 1900s for being a poor influence on children. ....

When TV came along, mass media became an even bigger influence. By 1955 approximately two-thirds of U.S. households owned a TV set. Within a few short decades, almost every family had a TV. Today visiting a movie theater or renting a DVD is a common experience. More and more channels and more ways to view movies or TV shows make it easier to access a variety of content. Cable and satellite technology, DVRs, online services such as

By the mid-1950s, the majority of U.S. homes had a TV set.

Netflix and Hulu, and portable devices all have expanded viewing capabilities.

While content has become easier to access, it also has become more graphic. Before the 1960s movies featured crime or other violent themes, but deaths were not shown realistically. For example, someone in a Western might be shown dying from a single bullet hole with no visible blood. That changed in 1967 when director Arthur Penn killed off the title characters of *Bonnie and Clyde* in a bloody, slow-motion scene. It may have looked mild by today's standards, but the level of gore was shocking at the time. Penn explained that he was influenced by media reports of the Vietnam War. He wanted to show the consequences of violence in a more realistic way.

The movie received mixed reviews in the media, but audiences loved it, and it won two Academy Awards. *Bonnie and Clyde* quickly paved the way for graphically violent movies such as *The Wild Bunch*, *Taxi Driver*, and *The Godfather*.

Since then special effects have continued to become more realistic. Movie studios continue to draw in audiences with violent fare. From realistic war movies, such as *Saving Private Ryan*, to violent action movies, such as *Kill Bill*, modern directors keep pushing the envelope of what they will show.

Introducing Interactive Entertainment

Initially video game graphics were extremely simple. For example, a spaceship might look like a mere triangle. Over the years graphics have become more realistic. Today games such as *Grand Theft Auto* and *Halo* have such realistic graphics and fluidly moving characters that the experience much more closely simulates real violence.

Kill Bill contained scenes that were so violent they switched from color to black and white for the movie to maintain its R rating.

The more realistic the violence becomes, the more urgent the questions seem about what effect it is having on viewers or players. At the same time violent forms of entertainment have become more accessible than ever before. Portable devices such as smartphones, MP3 players, and laptops have made it more difficult for adults to regulate what children see. A survey by the Pew Research Center found that 97 percent of kids ages 12 to 17 play video games either on a computer, gaming console, or portable device. Almost half of boys play video games on a

**The 1972 Atari video game *Pong* was very
different from the violent video games of today.**

cell phone or other handheld device. Popular genres
include racing, puzzle, action, and adventure games.

Economic realities also have changed. It has
become more difficult for some families to achieve
or maintain middle-class status. In many households
both parents work full-time. Many adults work
long hours. These changes have meant that some
children spend more time away from their parents,
in day care, in after-school activities, or elsewhere.
This can mean more exposure to pop culture, at

times without adult supervision. The result is that some children see more extreme violence at younger ages, with or without their parents' consent. Experts are still wrestling with what this means for society.

How are the concerns over violence in modern video games and movies similar to issues that were debated earlier in history? Has the problem become more serious, or does it only seem more serious? Should movies and video games depict violence realistically? What are the advantages and drawbacks of more advanced technology?

Economic realities have changed. It has become more difficult for some families to achieve or maintain middle-class status.

CHAPTER 3

VIEWING BLOOD AND GORE

> *"Maybe the love of violence is an integral part of human nature, undivorceable from our better selves. If so, it will continue to be a large part of our future entertainments as well as our history."*
>
> —Stephen King, best-selling author

When movies started showing more graphic violence in the 1960s, audiences reacted positively. *Bonnie and Clyde* set a box-office record when it was released in 1967. Movie studios started to realize the mass-market appeal of such movies. Action and horror movies continue to be among the most financially successful films. People seem to enjoy watching killing sprees, car chases, sword fights, shoot-outs, and other acts of violence. But why?

One theory is that people are drawn to violence in entertainment because it lets them release their own feelings of aggression in a socially acceptable manner. From the time children are very young, they are told not to hit or kick or hurt other people. They are punished when they do these things. Games and other forms of entertainment are a safe way to work out their feelings of aggression. Many younger children will act out scenarios such as cops and robbers or superheroes and villains. They might enjoy playing with toy guns or swords. Such imitative play is generally thought to be harmless. It is about acting out feelings of aggression or about feeling powerful. So the games are not seen as a problem in the same way as real violence, where the goal is to hurt or harm.

Children might be drawn to such types of entertainment because they are trying to understand something that is interesting to them. They also may be fascinated by behavior that is forbidden or intrigued by characters who seem to have power they lack. In the movie *Star Wars Episode I: The Phantom Menace*, Darth Maul was one of the most popular characters, despite only having five lines and little screen time. Many children dressed up as the villain for Halloween. Why? "It may be that it was because he was a virtually unstoppable force who answered to no one but himself," speculated Steven J. Kirsh, author of a book on media violence. "Darth Maul did not have to show restraint, and he did not have to eat his vegetables."

Emotional and Physical Reactions

Movies also are a way to face fears. You might think of them as roller coaster rides—a way to experience thrills without putting yourself in danger. Watching an action movie can actually have physical effects. Your blood pressure and heart rate can go up. Your body releases a chemical called adrenaline. The effect can be exciting or pleasurable. Even Disney movies contain elements

Movies also are a way to face fears. You might think of them as roller coaster rides—a way to experience thrills without putting yourself in danger.

Even movies geared toward families and young children often feature scenes of mild violence with characters in stressful situations. . . . .

of violence. In *Toy Story 3*, a popular 2010 movie that was rated G, the main characters get stuck in a garbage incinerator at a landfill and appear to be facing certain death. When the toys escape unharmed, the audience feels a sense of relief.

Sometimes conflicts that involve violence are appealing for other reasons. Many popular action movies contain a story of good versus evil. A likable hero defeats an enemy in the name of justice,

The *Star Wars* films feature many fight scenes between heroes and villains. · · · · · · · · · · · · · ·

creating a satisfying ending to a conflict. Some of the most gripping stories are ones that make you care about the characters and their experiences. Movies that show grotesque gore just for shock value are not necessarily enjoyable to everyone.

TOP 10 HIGHEST GROSSING MOVIES OF 2010

All of the 10 most popular movies of 2010 featured violence in some form. *Inception* and *Clash of the Titans* both contained typical action-movie violence. In *How to Train Your Dragon,* Vikings fought off dragons with swords and other weaponry in long battle scenes. *Shrek Forever After* had witches fighting ogres, and *Eclipse* showed werewolves battling vampires. Even the G-rated *Toy Story 3* showed toys in peril.

Source: The Hollywood Reporter

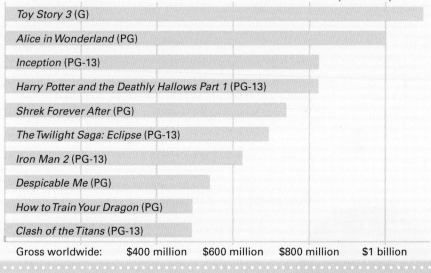

Toy Story 3 (G)			
Alice in Wonderland (PG)			
Inception (PG-13)			
Harry Potter and the Deathly Hallows Part 1 (PG-13)			
Shrek Forever After (PG)			
The Twilight Saga: Eclipse (PG-13)			
Iron Man 2 (PG-13)			
Despicable Me (PG)			
How to Train Your Dragon (PG)			
Clash of the Titans (PG-13)			

| Gross worldwide: | $400 million | $600 million | $800 million | $1 billion |

But when a character the audience has grown to identify with defeats an enemy, is injured, or is even killed, the emotional reaction can be powerful.

Sometimes media violence can strike audiences as fantastical. Often the producers of such entertainment will make the violence unrealistic enough that we don't react to it in the same way as we would if someone we knew was hurt or killed. In an action movie, a hero might survive despite numerous injuries, providing a clue that what is happening is fantasy. There may be few consequences shown. The audience might see the act of violence but not a prolonged or clear view of death or dying. Usually you will not see the friends or family of a slain villain mourning. Video games treat death in a similarly casual manner. A player racks up points and then moves on to the next goal. This helps keep entertainment enjoyable. But some fear that such casual treatment of violence could desensitize people to real-life violence.

Banking on Violence

When entertainment companies realized there was such a large market for action and horror movies and other graphic violence in entertainment, they stepped up to fill the demand. Some media executives have defended

Millions of fans worldwide saw *Harry Potter and the Deathly Hallows Part 2* on its opening night in 2011. In the United States alone the final Harry Potter film brought in nearly $170 million in its opening weekend. ....

their content by pointing out that violence is a part of real life. Others say they are merely giving audiences what they want.

The main goal of these companies is to make money. They have found that such projects are likely to be successful. Movies that feature extreme violence are more likely to make money than movies

Violent content can help the sales of a movie, but some people wonder if it is ethical to market action movies to younger viewers. Even if the movie is unrealistic, such as *Cowboys & Aliens*, some believe it can desensitize viewers to violence. . . . .

that do not. One reason action movies do so well is that they are easy to translate into other languages and therefore sell around the world. While one country's jokes might not be understood in another language, everyone understands bullets and car chases.

This rise in entertainment violence is not necessarily a bad thing. Violence often serves a purpose to drive the plot. If no crime were committed in a movie about the police force, there would be no mystery to be solved. The violence is pretend, so no one actually gets hurt. Still many people find the trend disturbing. They worry about its consequences.

Do you enjoy action or horror movies? How does it make you feel to see someone hurt or killed on-screen? Do think it is OK for entertainment companies to produce violent content? Do you agree that they are merely producing what audiences want, or should they take more responsibility for the content they provide? What do you think of the marketing practices of movie, music, and video game companies? Should they make a greater effort not to advertise to children? What do you think the consequences might be, if any, of a culture desensitized to violence?

CHAPTER 4

THE IMPACT OF MEDIA VIOLENCE

> "Kids today. So desensitized by movies and television."
>
> —The Grinch (played by Jim Carrey), after unsuccessfully trying to scare a small child in How the Grinch Stole Christmas

Researchers have conducted hundreds of studies to determine what effect exposure to media violence has on people, especially children. Some factors have made it difficult to prove a definite relationship. If someone viewed a violent action movie and immediately committed a similar act of violence, the effect would be obvious. However, increases in aggression may be the effect of repeated exposure over years. Aggressive attitudes or actions might not materialize until months or years later. Many experts view exposure to media violence as one factor among many that can lead to aggression. Other factors may include poverty, troubled family life, drug use, exposure to gang violence, or mental disorders. One study showed that children from low-income families spend significantly more time watching TV than their wealthier peers. This may lead to more exposure to violent programming.

In spite of these difficulties, many experts have found that exposure to violence in entertainment does affect people. Researchers have found that the influence of media violence on aggressive behavior has grown since 1975. This may be because of increased exposure or an increase in the graphic nature of entertainment violence. Numerous studies have identified short-term increases in aggressive tendencies after exposure to violent programming. A few studies also have found lasting effects. One study showed a link between heavy exposure to media

Mixed martial arts fighting is a popular form of entertainment. ....

violence at age 8 and increased aggressive behavior at age 19 among males.

In 2000 six large professional organizations issued a joint statement to Congress about the effects of media violence on children. Based on more than 1,000 studies, the organizations concluded that children who are exposed to media violence are more likely to:

- view violence as a valid solution to a dispute
- have a lesser emotional response to real-life violence and be less likely to help someone who is hurt
- see the world as a dangerous place and have a higher mistrust of other people
- be more likely to engage in aggressive behavior later in life.

The organizations issuing the statement were the American Medical Association, American Academy of Pediatrics, American Psychological Association, American Psychiatric Association, American Academy of Family Physicians, and the American Academy of Child & Adolescent Psychiatry.

Less research has been done on the effects of music containing violent lyrics. But some studies of college students have found that listening to such music leads to feelings of hostility afterward. Male students who listened to rap or heavy-metal music with violent lyrics felt

Less research has been done on the effects of music containing violent lyrics.

HAS VIOLENCE INCREASED?

In opposition to those who say the media's increasing obsession with violence leads to real-life violence, some people point to the fact that the rates of violent crime nationwide have mostly decreased in recent years. Preliminary data from the Federal Bureau of Investigation (FBI) for 2010 also shows a 6.2 percent decrease in crime compared with the previous year.

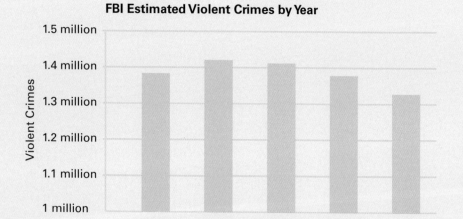

FBI Estimated Violent Crimes by Year

Source: Federal Bureau of Investigation

increased aggression toward women in the short term. Another study focused on the effects of music videos. Teens in three groups were shown a collection of violent rap videos, a group of videos

Some people associate rap artists, such as Eminem, with violence and gang activity. ·

with no violence, or no videos at all. They then were asked to react to a character in a story. Students who viewed the first group of videos were the most likely to support violence against the character.

Studies of video games have had similar results. College students who played violent video games experienced several short-term side effects. They were more likely to experience aggressive thoughts, feelings, and behavior after playing. In a study of 9- to 12-year-olds, children were divided into two groups that each played a game rated E (appropriate for everyone) for 20 minutes. One group played games featuring cartoon characters attacking nonhuman enemies. The other group played a nonviolent game. Afterward children from both groups played a game in which players selected how severely to punish an opponent. Members of

DANGERS OF IMITATION

Children, particularly young children, learn through observation and are likely to imitate what they see. Studies have shown that children who see physical aggression, such as kicking, hitting, or biting, are more likely to engage in those behaviors. Sometimes children may engage in violence without understanding the consequences of their actions.

In 1999 a 12-year-old wrestling fan beat a 6-year-old girl to death. Defense lawyers argued that he was imitating the moves of his favorite wrestlers and did not understand that he was hurting her. The jury found the boy guilty. The trial reawakened discussion of the dangers of media violence.

the group who had just played the more violent game punished their opponents at higher levels than members of the second group.

Theories on Aggressive Behavior

Several decades ago researchers attempted to prove the catharsis theory—that violent forms of entertainment had a positive effect on people. Some believed that if players or viewers released their negative feelings or aggressive theories by engaging in fantasy, they were less likely to engage in real aggression. Many other researchers later disproved these initial studies.

The most common theory today about the effects of media violence is called social learning theory. It says that children learn through observing and then imitating behavior. This can include behaviors they see in real life as well as on TV. Research has shown that children are more likely to copy behaviors they see being rewarded, while avoiding behaviors that they see punished. They also are more likely to mimic characters who they see as similar to themselves. This theory is used to explain how young children acquire aggressive

Children who witness media violence may be more likely to copy the violent behaviors they see on TV or in video games.

tendencies. Field experiments have shown this theory to have merit. In one study, for example, children who were shown violent cartoons were then more likely to be aggressive with their peers in social situations. This effect has been seen for both animated and live-action shows.

VIOLENCE IN TELEVISION

The National Television Violence Study reported on what kinds of programs contain the most violence. It evaluated programs on 23 channels, including network TV, premium cable channels, and Public Broadcasting Service (PBS). Violence was found in:

- 60 percent of all programming
- 100 percent of slapstick cartoons (such as *The Bugs Bunny Show*)
- 97 percent of superhero cartoons
- 90 percent of televised movies
- 84 percent of premium cable shows
- 70 percent of dramas
- 69 percent of children's programming
- 63 percent of basic cable shows
- 57 percent of non-children's programming
- 51 percent of broadcast network shows
- 35 percent of comedy and reality shows
- 18 percent of PBS shows

Another theory of how media affect people is called priming theory. It says a violent game, movie, or song can trigger aggressive thoughts or feelings. The person then is "primed" for aggressive behavior. The effect is especially pronounced when something in real life resembles something from the mode of entertainment. One study, for example, found that students who had just seen a violent movie were more likely to mistreat a student with the same name as a villain from the movie immediately after seeing it.

A fourth theory relates to information processing. When the brain sees a scenario play out in a certain way over time, it develops a script for how that scenario should play out. Based on what it has observed, the mind keeps action plans to respond to these events. If a child repeatedly sees violence being used as a solution to a problem, either in real life or entertainment, the use of violence becomes a script. Over time, the theory says, the child becomes more likely to use aggression as a solution to problems.

Counterargument

Some experts think the negative effects of media violence have been overblown. Karen Sternheimer, a sociologist who has studied and written about the issue extensively, is one such expert. She pointed out that while exposure to violence through various forms of entertainment

Some experts think the negative effects of media violence have been overblown.

Even children's cartoons featuring popular characters, such as Wile E. Coyote and Road Runner, can depict acts of violence.

has expanded, real violence has declined in the past several decades.

From 1997 to 2006, violent crimes committed by juveniles declined by 20 percent. In 2006 nine children ages 6 to 12 were arrested for homicide, which was the lowest number of arrests for that age group since statistics started being kept in 1964.

Some experts also have pointed out that the people who use the most media are not the ones who commit the most violent crimes. Children from

Experts disagree about whether violence in the media leads to real-life acts of violence. Low-income areas typically have higher crime rates. However, kids growing up in these environments usually have less access to many kinds of media than kids in high-income areas. · · · · · · · · · · · · · · · ·

higher-income families have access to more forms of media. They see more movies and play more video games, for example. When a severe crime occurs in a high-income area, it usually receives lots of news coverage because it is so unusual. However, crime rates are higher among people with lower incomes, and less access to a wide variety of media.

Members of the media industries in question also have stepped forward to defend themselves. The Entertainment Software Association (ESA) dedicates a section of its website to addressing violence in video games. It cites the fact that real-life violence has decreased as video games have gained popularity. The ESA questions the accuracy of studies that have shown a link between violence in video games and violent behavior. Its website also cites a number of researchers and authors who have supported this view.

The ESA questions the accuracy of studies that have shown a link between violence in video games and violent behavior.

Do you agree that exposure to violent entertainment makes people more aggressive? Has that been your experience? What other factors make people more or less likely to show aggression? How do you feel after playing a violent video game or seeing an action movie? Is it possible that viewing violence in media can actually decrease violent actions?

CHAPTER 5

THE RESPONSE TO AGGRESSION

> "I don't like the ones that glorify antisocial behavior, like Grand Theft Auto and Vice City. We actually had a rule at Atari, which seems kind of quaint now, that you could blow up a tank, a plane, a car—but you couldn't do violence against a human."
>
> —Nolan Bushnell, creator of the early gaming system Atari

While most research shows some short- and long-term effects of violence, what should be done about it is another matter. Many people view this as an important issue that needs addressing. At times politicians and members of the public have pressured the movie and video game industries to rein in violent content or at least to stop marketing it to children.

The First Amendment to the U.S. Constitution guarantees a right to free speech and expression.

While many people see violence as entertainment as a societal problem, the First Amendment limits what the government can do to address it. The industries behind such content have responded to public pressure with efforts to self-regulate. They set their own rules and ratings systems.

The Motion Picture Association of America (MPAA) has a ratings system that gives people an idea of what movies are appropriate for various age groups. The ratings, which are determined by a board of parents, are based on the amount of sex, violence, and inappropriate language in a movie. A rating of G (for general) means a movie is OK for anyone to watch, while PG means that parental guidance is suggested. PG-13 means a

Disney's *Pirates of the Caribbean* series was originally based on a Disneyland ride, but all the movies have a PG-13 rating and feature scenes of sword fighting and other violence. · · · · · · · · · · · · · · · ·

movie may not be suitable for anyone under age 13. Children under the age of 17 are not supposed to be admitted to movies rated R unless accompanied by a

ACCESS TO RESTRICTED MOVIES AND GAMES

In studying the marketing practices of entertainment companies, the Federal Trade Commission (FTC) conducted an experiment to see how easily underage children could gain admission into movies rated R. By simply lying about their ages at the box office, 39 percent of participants were able to gain admission. R-rated DVDs or an unrated version of a movie that received an R rating for its theatrical version were successfully purchased by 71 percent of children. Often unrated versions are director's cuts that would be rated NC-17.

parent or adult guardian, and NC-17 means no one under 17 should be admitted.

Movie studios do not have to submit their movies to the MPAA for review. A movie that is not reviewed is simply listed as unrated. Some movies have theatrical versions that are rated, as well as an unrated version that is available only on DVD. The unrated version may contain additional content that is inappropriate for minors. The MPAA also reviews advertising materials for each movie it reviews to make sure they are appropriate for the audience that will view the advertisements. This is to ensure that an audience

The Entertainment Software Ratings Board assigns ratings to video games. The ratings are prominently featured on the cover of the game case.

for a G-rated movie doesn't see a trailer featuring R-rated content, for example.

The video game industry has developed its own system of ratings. It is voluntary, but almost all games in the United States go through the rating process. The Entertainment Software Ratings Board (ESRB) assigns the ratings. The ratings include EC (early childhood), E (everyone), E10+ (everyone age 10 and up), T (teen), M (mature), and AO (adults only). Rated games feature a symbol for the rating, as well as content indicators on the back cover that show the reason for the assigned rating. Some content indicators include "animated blood," "comic mischief," and "fantasy violence." The ESRB also has guidelines for the acceptable marketing practices for rated games. It is up to retailers to regulate the sale of rated games to minors.

The music industry does not have an extensive rating system, but it does have a warning label that is applied to some albums. The label reads, "Parental Advisory: Explicit Content." It may be used on music containing references to drug use, sex, violence, or inappropriate language. It does not include any indication of why a particular piece of music was labeled as such.

Marketing Violence to Children

A 2000 Federal Trade Commission study discovered that companies were actively marketing movies, music, and video games containing inappropriate content to children and teens. The

Even with ratings for video games in place, many children and teenagers play games that are rated M or AO. However, in a 2008 survey, only a small number of teens chose games rated M or AO for all of their top three favorite games.

Number of M/AO Rated Games by Gender among Teens Who Play Any M/AO Rated Games

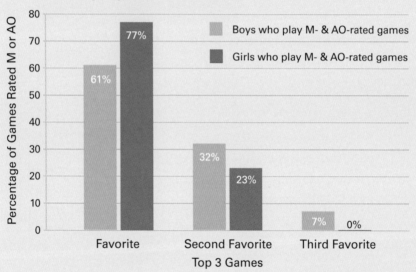

Source: Pew Internet and American Life Project

FTC's year-long study found that marketing plans for R-rated movies—those that are supposed to admit ages 17 and up—were made to appeal to children as young as 12. Some companies were

Even if a violent game is rated M (mature), the company that makes it may still try to market it to a younger audience by using advertising targeted toward that age demographic.

making websites to promote the films with features that appealed to teens. Some showed clips of R-rated movies during kid-friendly shows such as MTV's *Total Request Live*.

The study also found that some music and video games containing warning labels for explicit content or a mature rating were being marketed to children. For example, the marketing plan for one game with a mature rating for graphic violence identified the primary target audience as males ages 12 to 17. The secondary audience was males ages 18 to 34. The company planned to reach the younger age group through magazines and TV shows popular among teenage boys.

Following the report, entertainment companies responded to public pressure by committing to changing their marketing practices. The FTC did follow-up studies in 2007 and 2009, finding that most companies no longer explicitly identified teens as a target market for adult content. But in violation of industry standards, some products that were rated R or M were still being advertised during children's TV programs and on websites catering to children. The movie industry does not have any rule against marketing PG-13 movies to children under age 13. The FTC report encouraged the adoption of such a rule, which would also restrict tie-in marketing of inappropriate movies to toys and kids' meals. The FTC also noted that ratings are not highly visible on DVD cases. The increasing number of unrated versions of movies

The FTC did follow-up studies in 2007 and 2009, finding that most companies no longer explicitly identified teens as a target market for adult content.

Younger children are more likely to buy *Iron Man* action figures than the teens who are old enough to see the film based on its PG-13 rating.

released on DVD has led to confusion about some movies' content.

The music industry has not yet adopted marketing guidelines. According to the FTC, music that has been assigned a warning label for explicit content is still advertised during TV shows popular among teens. The warning label frequently is not visible or is hard to read in commercials or other ads.

What's the Big Deal?

Not everyone agrees that media violence is an issue requiring urgent attention. Some experts see it as one factor among many that contributes to violence in society. They think violence in the media is getting too much attention, while more complicated or controversial problems are not addressed. Karen Sternheimer wrote about this possibility in her book, *Connecting Social Problems and Popular Culture: Why Media Is Not the Answer*. Many real-life factors, Sternheimer wrote, can influence the lives of troubled children and make them more likely to become violent. They include lack of sufficient food and shelter, inadequate education, and absent or abusive parents.

In 2011 approximately

Not everyone agrees that media violence is an issue requiring urgent attention.

An estimated one in every five children lives in poverty. Many experts consider this a much more serious contributor to violent behavior than the media.

15.5 million American children were living in poverty. That amounted to just under one-fifth of all children. "The most pressing crisis facing American children today is not media culture, but poverty," Sternheimer wrote. "By continually hyping the fear of media made child killers, we forget that the biggest threat to childhood is adults and the policies that adults create."

Research has shown that more parental involvement in a child's life often makes the child less likely to exhibit violent behavior—even if the child enjoys violent video games or movies. · · · · · · · · · · · ·

In the report *Grand Theft Childhood*, researchers concluded that video game content seemed to be one factor among many that influenced children's behavior. Cheryl K. Olson and Larry Kutner conducted a study of video game violence that was funded by the U.S. Department of Justice. They noted that some children might be at higher risk of being affected than others. Children who already had an aggressive personality, came from a troubled home or neighborhood, had low parental involvement, or had learning delays seemed to experience more negative effects from video games. But for most children, Olson and Kutner said, video games are a normal and harmless form of entertainment.

They wrote: "Focusing on such easy but minor targets as violent video games causes parents, social activists and public policy makers to ignore the much more powerful and significant causes of youth violence that have already been well established, including a range of social, behavioral, economic, biological and

Children who already had an aggressive personality, came from a troubled home or neighborhood, had low parental involvement, or had learning delays seemed to experience more negative effects from video games.

A study evaluated several dozen video games that were rated E (acceptable for everyone). Of these, approximately two-thirds featured physical aggression, and one-third included violence. In approximately two-thirds of the games studied, players advanced to the next level by injuring other players. Another study looked at games rated T (appropriate for teens). Of these, almost all contained violence. On average, approximately one-third of playing time was spent engaged in violence. Almost all the games rewarded players for violent acts.

mental health factors. In other words, the knee-jerk responses distract us from more complex but more important problems."

What Do You Think?

Do you think that violence as entertainment is a problem that needs addressing? Are we currently focusing too much, too little, or not enough attention on the issue? Are ratings systems effective? Are they helpful? What problems do you see with the ratings systems today? What could you do as a consumer to address violence in entertainment?

Video game ratings are in place to help keep violent and other inappropriate materials away from young gamers.

Will your knowledge about the potential effects of media violence affect your entertainment choices in the future?

Here are some exercises that will help you consider the effects of violence in the media:

1 Watch an age-appropriate movie that features some sort of violence, and think about the following:

What purpose does the violence serve in the plot of the movie?

How would the movie be different if there were more or less violence?

Is the violence portrayed realistically?

What emotional reactions did you have to the violence?

2 Watch a 30-minute cartoon geared toward young children.

How many instances of violence did you count?

How did this violence differ from the violence in a movie or TV show geared toward older audiences?

How would the cartoon be different if there were more or less violence? Would it be as entertaining?

3 While you're watching TV, keep a notebook nearby. Make a check mark every time you see an act of aggression or violence on-screen.

How many check marks do you have after an hour?

Does the number surprise you?

4 If you enjoy playing video games, keep a journal for a week. Every time you finish playing a game, make a quick note of what sort of game you played and what you felt like when you were done. After a week review what you wrote.

Did the games seem to affect your mood afterward?

Did games that involved some sort of violence make you feel differently than other games?

GLOSSARY

alienated
caused to be withdrawn or unfriendly

aggression
forceful action or words

arsenal
storehouse of weapons and ammunition

catharsis
release of emotions

communism
system in which goods and property are owned by the government and shared in common

controversial
causing dispute or disagreement

desensitize
to become emotionally detached or callous

graphic
extremely, and perhaps unnecessarily, lifelike or realistic

grotesque
very strange or ugly

hostility
feelings of ill will

integral
necessary to make complete

opinion piece
a written article that states the writer's point of view on a subject

paranoia
a tendency toward excessive distrust

scapegoat
something that blame is placed on when it is not deserved

scrutiny
an intense study or inspection

self-regulation
setting rules for oneself

vulnerable
capable of being physically or emotionally wounded

Investigate Further

Merino, Noel. *Media Violence.*
Farmington Hills, Mich.: Greenhaven, 2010.

Nagle, Jeanne. *Violence in Movies, Music, and the Media.*
New York: Rosen, 2008.

Rosinsky, Natalie M. *Graphic Content!: The Culture of Comic Books.*
Mankato, Minn.: Compass Point Books, 2010.

Internet Sites

Use FactHound to find Internet sites related to this book. All of the sites on FactHound have been researched by our staff.

Here's all you do:

Visit *www.facthound.com*

Type in this code: 9780756545208

Keep Exploring Media Literacy!

Read the other books in this series:

The Big Push: *How Popular Culture Is Always Selling*
Choosing News: *What Gets Reported and Why*
Selling Ourselves: *Marketing Body Images*

SOURCE NOTES

Chapter 1

Page 4, opening quote: Douglas A. Gentile, ed. *Media Violence and Children: A Complete Guide for Parents and Professionals*. Westport, Conn.: Praeger, 2003, p. 8.

Page 5, line 10: Ibid., pp. 4–5.

Page 7, line 15: John Leo. "When Life Imitates Video." *U.S. News and World Report*. 25 April 1999. 3 June 2011. www.usnews.com/usnews/opinion/articles/990503/archive_000875.htm

Page 9, sidebar, line 4: "The Final Report and Findings of the Safe School Initiative." United States Secret Service. 5 June 2011.www.secretservice.gov/ntac_ssi.shtml

Page 10, line 12: Gina Kolata. "A Study Finds More Links Between TV and Violence." *The New York Times*. 29 March 2002. 19 Aug. 2011. www.nytimes.com/2002/03/29/us/a-study-finds-more-links-between-tv-and-violence.html

Page 12, graph: "Teens, Video Games, and Civics." Pew Internet and American Life Project. 16 Sept. 2008. 25 May 2011. www.pewinternet.org/~/media//Files/Reports/2008/PIP_Teens_Games_and_Civics_Report_FINAL.pdf.pdf

Page 15, line 7: Marilyn Manson. "Whose Fault Is It?" *Rolling Stone*. 24 June 1999, p. 23.

Page 17, line 12: Karen Sternheimer. *Connecting Social Problems and Popular Culture: Why Media Is Not the Answer.* Boulder, Colo.: Westview Press, 2010, pp. 76–77.

Page 17, line 21: *Media Violence and Children: A Complete Guide for Parents and Professionals*, p. 16. Page 19, sidebar, line 7: Sandra L. Calvert and Barbara J. Wilson, eds. *The Handbook of Children, Media, and Development*. Chichester, U.K.: Wiley-Blackwell, 2011, pp. 239–240.

Chapter 2

Page 22, opening quote: *Media Violence and Children: A Complete Guide for Parents and Professionals,* p. 1.

Page 28, line 2: Steven J. Kirsh. *Children, Adolescents, and Media Violence: A Critical Look at the Research*. Thousand Oaks, Calif.: Sage Publications, 2006, p. 7.

Page 31, line 8: "Teens, Video Games, and Civics."

Chapter 3

Page 34, opening quote: Stephen King. "A History of Violence." *Entertainment Weekly*. 7 Oct. 2007. 18 May 2011. www.ew.com/ew/article/0,,20150871,00.html

Page 34, line 5: Peter Biskand. *Gods and Monsters: Thirty Years of Writing on Film and Culture from One of America's Most Incisive Writers*. New York: Nation Books, 2004, p. 118.

Page 36, line 7: *Children, Adolescents, and Media Violence: A Critical Look at the Research*, p. 85.

Page 39, graph: Pamela McClintock. "Top 10 Highest Grossing Films of 2010." *The Hollywood Reporter*. 24 Dec. 2010. 13 Sept. 2011. www.hollywoodreporter.com/gallery/top-10-grossing-films-2010-65349#1

Chapter 4

Page 44, opening quote: "Media Quotes: A Collection of Comments on the State of Entertainment." Parents Television Council. 6 June 2011. www.parentstv.org/PTC/facts/mediaquotes.asp

Page 45, line 2: Mary Kay Fox and Nancy Cole. *Nutrition and Health Characteristics of Low-income Populations: Volume 1, Food Stamp Program Participants and Nonparticipants*. United States Department of Agriculture. 1 Dec. 2004. 19 Aug. 2011. www.ers.usda.gov/Publications/EFAN04014-1/

Page 45, line 9: *Media Violence and Children: A Complete Guide for Parents and Professionals*, p. 213. Page 45, line 13: Ibid., p. 85.

Page 45, line 16: Ibid., p. 69.

Page 46, line 3: "Joint Statement on the Impact of Entertainment Violence on Children Congressional Public Health Summit July 26, 2000." American Academy of Pediatrics. 9 Aug. 2011. www.aap.org/advocacy/releases/jstmtevc.htm

Page 48, graph: "Crime in the United States." Federal Bureau of Investigation. 13 Sept. 2011. www2.fbi.gov/ucr/cius2009/offenses/violent_crime/index.html

Page 48, line 2: *Media Violence and Children: A Complete Guide for Parents and Professionals*, p. 168.

Page 49, line 5: *The Handbook of Children, Media, and Development*, pp. 252–253.

Page 50, sidebar, line 4: *Media Violence and Children: A Complete Guide for Parents and Professionals*, p. 108.

Page 51, line 19: *Children, Adolescents, and Media Violence: A Critical Look at the Research*, p. 54.

Page 52, line 1: *The Handbook of Children, Media, and Development*, p. 251.

Page 53, sidebar, line 1: Ibid., p. 239.

Page 54, line 1: Ibid., p. 256.

Page 55, line 3: *Connecting Social Problems and Popular Culture: Why Media is Not the Answer*, pp. 81–83.

Chapter 5

Page 58, opening quote: "Media Quotes: A Collection of Comments on the State of Entertainment."

Page 61, sidebar, line 1: "Marketing Violent Entertainment to Children." Federal Trade Commission. April 2007. 20 May 2011. www.gamecensorship.com/FTCReportMarketingViolencetoChildren.pdf

Page 63, line 21: "FTC Issues Report on Marketing Violent Entertainment to Children." Federal Trade Commission. 12 April 2001. 8 Aug. 2011. www.ftc.gov/opa/2007/04/marketingviolence.shtm

Page 64, graph: "Teens, Video Games, and Civics."

Page 66, line 8: *Children, Adolescents, and Media Violence: A Critical Look at the Research*, pp. 291–292.

Page 68, line 23: "The State of America's Children 2011 Report." Children's Defense Fund. 8 Aug. 2011. www.childrensdefense.org/child-research-data-publications/state-of-americas-children-2011/

Page 69, line 2: *Connecting Social Problems and Popular Culture: Why Media is Not the Answer*, p. 3.

Page 71, line 15: "Games & Violence." Entertainment Software Association. 5 June 2011. www.theesa.com/facts/violence.asp

Page 72, sidebar, line 1: *The Handbook of Children, Media, and Development*, p. 243.

SELECT BIBLIOGRAPHY

Calvert, Sandra L., and Barbara J. Wilson, eds. *The Handbook of Children, Media, and Development*. Chichester, U.K.: Wiley-Blackwell, 2011.

Gentile, Douglas A., ed. *Media Violence and Children: A Complete Guide for Parents and Professionals*. Westport, Conn.: Praeger, 2003.

Goldstein, Jeffrey H., ed. *Why We Watch: The Attractions of Violent Entertainment*. New York: Oxford University Press, 1998.

Kirsh, Steven J. *Children, Adolescents, and Media Violence: A Critical Look at the Research*. Thousand Oaks, Calif.: Sage Publications, 2006.

Sternheimer, Karen. *Connecting Social Problems and Popular Culture: Why Media Is Not the Answer*. Boulder, Colo.: Westview Press, 2010.

INDEX

ABOUT THE AUTHOR

Erika Wittekind is a freelance writer and editor based in Wisconsin. She has covered education and government for several community newspapers, winning an award for best local news story from the Minnesota Newspaper Association for 2002.